# Jean Lafitte

## Pirate-Hero of the War of 1812

Aileen Weintraub

The Rosen Publishing Group's
## PowerKids Press™
New York

JB LAFITTE

*To my DaddyMonster, who was the most fearless of them all*

Published in 2002 by The Rosen Publishing Group, Inc.
29 East 21st Street, New York, NY 10010

First Edition

Book Design: Michael Caroleo and Michael de Guzman
Layout: Nick Sciacca
Project Editors: Jennifer Landau, Jason Moring, Jennifer Quasha

Consultant: Ken Kinkor

Photo credits: p. 4 (treasure) © Christie's Images Ltd.; pp. 4, 12, 19, 20 © North Wind Pictures; pp. 7, 8, 15 by Mica Angela Fulgium; p.11 (Lafitte) © Bettmann/CORBIS; p. 11 (bayou) © Robert Holmes/CORBIS; p. 11 (map) © MapArt; 16 © Bettmann/CORBIS.

Weintraub, Aileen, 1973–
    Jean Lafitte / Aileen Weintraub. —1st ed.
        p. cm. — (The library of the pirates)
Includes index.
 ISBN 0–8239–5796–9
1. Lafitte, Jean—Juvenile literature. 2. Pirates—Louisiana—Biography—Juvenile literature. 3. Pirates—Texas—Biography—Juvenile literature. 4. New Orleans (La.), Battle of, 1815—Juvenile literature. 5. Privateering—Mexico, Gulf of—History—nineteenth century—Juvenile literature. [1. Lafitte, Jean. 2. Pirates.] I. Title.
    F374.L2 W45 2002
    973.5'239'092—dc21
                                        00–01219

Manufactured in the United States of America

# Contents

1    From Blacksmith to Privateer    5

2    The Slave Trade    6

3    The Kingdom of Barataria    9

4    A Man Without a Country    10

5    The War of 1812    13

6    The British Make an Offer    14

7    The Battle of New Orleans    17

8    The Hero of New Orleans    18

9    After the Battle    21

10    The Legendary Lafitte    22

Glossary    23

Index    24

Web Sites    24

# From Blacksmith to Privateer

Many historians believe that the pirate Jean Lafitte was born in France in the 1780s. After moving to New Orleans, Louisiana, in the early 1800s, Lafitte and his brother opened a **blacksmith** shop. This business did not make the brothers enough money. Lafitte became a **privateer** for countries that asked for his help. Instead of payment, privateers took a share of the **booty** they stole from enemy ships. Lafitte **plundered** ships off the Caribbean coast and in the Atlantic Ocean. Pirating was illegal, but privateering was not. It was hard to tell the difference between a pirate and a privateer. This made it hard for anyone to arrest Lafitte.

▶ *Jean Lafitte did not like to be thought of as a pirate. He was a charming, well-dressed man.*

# The Slave Trade

In 1808, Lafitte and his brother began **smuggling** slaves. He used his blacksmith shop as a fake business to cover for his smuggling business. He brought slaves from Cuba for a small price and then sold them at a much higher one. Lafitte also kept plundering ships on the Gulf of Mexico. He would come back to Louisiana and sell cloths, linens, furniture, and spices at a cheap price. His business did so well that it threatened other merchants in New Orleans. New Orleans governor William C. C. Claiborne accused him of piracy. He posted a $500 reward for Lafitte's capture. In return, Lafitte posted a $1,500 reward for Claiborne's capture. There was nothing the governor could do to get rid of Jean Lafitte.

Jean Lafitte spent a lot of time hiding from the law. Once he even sank one of his own ships to avoid getting caught.

Many men helped Lafitte smuggle goods through the swamps and bayous of Louisiana. If a man stole anything, he was whipped.

# The Kingdom of Barataria

Jean Lafitte needed help with his smuggling business. He moved his headquarters to an island called Grande Terre in Barataria Bay, 50 miles (81 km) south of New Orleans. He had 1,000 men helping him smuggle goods through the swamps and **bayous** of Louisiana. Grande Terre was a pirate's paradise. The only way to get on and off the island was by boat. The men living there had all they could ever hope for, including food, money, and fine clothes. Lafitte told the men that if they obeyed the rules and performed their duties, they could live on Grande Terre as long as they wished. Barataria Bay became known as Lafitte's kingdom.

# A Man Without a Country

Lafitte was good at **navigating** through the swamps and bayous surrounding Barataria Bay. This made it hard for ships to catch him or get to his island. Lafitte was not American, but he respected the American way of life. He had a saying, "Attack an American ship and die." This was because he did not want the United States to attack his island. Even though the government didn't like him, the people of New Orleans were happy to buy goods from him. The U.S. government did a bad job taking care of the people in New Orleans. They didn't know how to navigate the swampy land. They also didn't understand the **Cajun** and **Creole** cultures of the people living there. Lafitte understood the people and cultures of New Orleans.

# New Orleans

Jean Lafitte, shown in the photo at left, sold many goods to the people of New Orleans.

This is a picture of the bayous of louisiana, which became a state in 1812.

This painting shows American soldiers firing at the
British from behind a wall.

# The War of 1812

In the early 1800s, there was a war between Great Britain and France. Neither country wanted the United States to trade with its enemy. Both sides put up **blockades** stopping trade to each other's ports. This harmed trade routes. Britain began attacking American ships. In June 1812, President James Madison declared war on Britain. The British wanted to gain control of the Mississippi River. To do this, they would have to attack the United States from the south, through the Gulf of Mexico and New Orleans. Jean Lafitte believed that the U.S. government would need his help.

# The British Make an Offer

In 1814, the British offered Jean Lafitte $30,000 and a position as captain in the Royal Navy if he would help them beat the Americans. The British asked Lafitte because he knew how to travel through the swampy bayou. Lafitte refused the offer. Governor Claiborne of New Orleans put out an arrest warrant for Lafitte, however, because he thought Lafitte was going to help the British. Lafitte told the American authorities about the offer that the British had made. They thought Lafitte was making up the story. The U.S. Navy attacked and destroyed Lafitte's home on Grande Terre Island. Lafitte and his men were surprised by the attack, but most of them escaped.

British officers came to Grande Terre to ask Lafitte for his help in the war against the Americans. Lafitte refused to help the British.

# The Battle of New Orleans

Edward Livingston, Lafitte's **attorney**, convinced the United States that the British really did make an offer to Lafitte. Lafitte agreed to help the Americans if the government **pardoned** him and his men for all of their past crimes. At first, General Andrew Jackson wasn't sure that he trusted Lafitte. Jackson didn't have much choice. Even with Lafitte's men, the British still would outnumber the American troops. The people of New Orleans began to panic because the British were going to attack. Every man over the age of 15 had to fight. On January 7, 1815, when the British appeared with 7,000 troops, the Battle of New Orleans began.

*This is a painting of the Battle of New Orleans. On December 17, 1814, Lafitte and his men were asked to help the Americans fight against the British.*

# The Hero of New Orleans

Lafitte rounded up his men from Barataria Bay. The British troops marched straight for the American troops. Three thousand American guns fired. The British troops began falling dead over one another. After only 1 hour, the British retreated. The number of British soldiers killed totaled 2,600. Only 13 American soldiers had died. Lafitte's warning that the British were going to attack and his help saved New Orleans from being destroyed. President James Madison gave Lafitte and his men a pardon and granted them **citizenship**. Although Lafitte was a hero, the War of 1812 had been over for more than a month. A **treaty** had been signed overseas, but there had been no quick way to get word of it to America.

This painting shows the Americans celebrating their victory in the Battle of New Orleans.

*Jean Lafitte was named the governor of Galveston Island in 1819.*

# After the Battle

Lafitte grew tired of living in New Orleans after the war. He also wanted back the goods that had been taken by the U.S. government when Grande Terre was destroyed. The government refused. They said that these goods were illegal and had been taken from him while he was a pirate. Lafitte was angry. In 1817, he left New Orleans and settled on Galveston Island off the coast of Texas. The people of Galveston wanted **independence** from Spain. Lafitte agreed to help Galveston by plundering Spanish ships. For a while, Lafitte was happy. In time, however, President James Madison declared war on pirates. Lafitte was ordered to leave Galveston. He gave up without a fight, setting fire to his town before sailing off.

# The Legendary Lafitte

No one knows for sure when or where Jean Lafitte died. While he was alive, many people both feared and respected him. It is said that treasure hunters who look for Lafitte's lost treasure along the Gulf of Mexico encounter a ghost that always leads them to the wrong spot. Some treasure hunters say a big snake with sharp fangs appears if anyone gets too close to Lafitte's buried treasure. Another story tells of a scary skeleton holding a huge sword which stands guard over Lafitte's gold. Many books have been written and movies have been made about this **legendary** pirate who helped the United States win an important battle. Today there is a national park named for him in Louisiana.

# Glossary

**attorney** (uh-TUR-nee)  A person who knows the laws and goes to court to prove that someone has committed a crime or to defend a person's actions.

**bayous** (BY-ooz)  Marshy or swampy bodies of water.

**blacksmith** (BLAK-smith)  A person who makes and repairs iron objects.

**blockades** (blah-KAYDS)  Ships that block passage to ports by ships of another country.

**booty** (BOO-tee)  Prizes stolen by force.

**Cajun** (KAY-jun)  A person from Louisiana who is descended from French immigrants.

**citizenship** (SIH-tih-zen-ship)  The legal right to live in a certain country.

**Creole** (KREE-ohl)  A white person who lives in the Gulf states and is descended from early French or Spanish settlers.

**independence** (in-dih-PEN-dints)  Freedom from the control of others.

**legendary** (LEH-jin-der-ee)  To be famous and important.

**navigating** (NAH-vuh-gayt-ing)  Knowing in which direction to travel.

**pardoned** (PAR-dind)  To excuse someone of an offense.

**plundered** (PLUN-derd)  To have robbed by force.

**privateer** (pry-vuh-TEER)  An armed pirate licensed by the government to attack enemy ships.

**smuggling** (SMUH-gling)  Sneaking something into or out of a country to avoid taxes.

**treaty** (TREE-tee)  A formal agreement, signed and agreed upon by each party.

# Index

**B**

Barataria Bay, 9, 10, 18
Battle of New Orleans, 17
bayous, 9, 10
blacksmith, 5, 6
blockades, 13
booty, 5

**C**

Cajun, 10
citizenship, 18
Claiborne, William C. C., 6, 14
Creole, 10

**F**

France, 5, 13

**G**

Galveston Island, 21
Grand Terre Island, 9, 14, 21
Great Britain, 13

**J**

Jackson, General Andrew, 17

**L**

Livingston, Edward, 17

**M**

Madison, President James, 13, 18, 21

**N**

New Orleans, Louisiana, 5, 6, 9, 10, 13, 14, 17, 18, 21

**P**

pirate, 5, 21
plundering, 5, 6, 21
privateer, 5

**S**

slaves, 6
smuggling, 6, 9
Spain, 21

**U**

United States, 10, 13, 17, 22

**W**

War of 1812, 18

# Web Sites

To learn more about Jean Lafitte, check out this Web site:
http://crimelibrary.com/americana/lafitte/main.htm